DAYS THAT SHOOK THE WORLD

TIANANMEN SQUARE

JUNE 4, 1989

Jane Bingham

Raintree

Chicago, Illinois

DAYS THAT SHOOK THE WORLD

Assassination in Sarajevo	The Invasion of Kuwait
The Chernobyl Disaster	The Kennedy Assassination
D-Day	The Moon Landing
The Dream of Martin Luther King	Pearl Harbor
The Fall of the Berlin Wall	The Russian Revolution
The Freeing of Nelson Mandela	Tiananmen Square
Hiroshima	The Wall Street Crash

For information, address the publisher:
Raintree, 100 N. LaSalle, Suite 1200, Chicago, IL 60602

Printed in Hong Kong by Wing King Tong.

08 07 06 05 04
10 9 8 7 6 5 4 3 2 1

Library of Congress Cataloging-in-Publication Data:

Bingham, Jane.
Tiananmen Square / Jane Bingham.
p. cm. -- (Days that shook the world) Audience: Ages 10-12 Includes index.
Contents: Protest in the square -- Emperors and peasants -- Mao's China -- Deng's China -- Changing times -- Voices of protest -- A hard winter: 1988-1989 -- The protest begins: April 1989 -- An anniversary and a visit -- The government takes action -- A goddess arrives -- The army moves closer -- Crackdown: June 4, 1989 -- Days of terror -- The trouble spreads -- The world reacts -- Changes in China -- What if? -- Legacy.
ISBN 0-7398-6649-4 (Library Binding-hardcover)
1. China--History--Tiananmen Square Incident, 1989--Juvenile literature. [1. China--History--Tiananmen Square Incident, 1989.] I. Title. II. Series.

DS779.32.B56 2004
951.05'8--dc22

2003012525

Cover picture: A student in Tiananmen Square challenges the driver of a tank to run him down.

Title page picture: Students in Shanghai take part in a nationwide protest in December 1986.

We are grateful to the following for permission to reproduce photographs:
Alamy 39 bottom (View Stock); Associated Press 31 bottom; Camera Press 17 top left (W. McQuitty); Corbis *front cover* (Bettmann), 6 (Peter Turnley), 7 (Peter Turnley), 14 (Tod Gipstein), 18 (Peter Turnley), 21 (Peter Turnley), 28 (Jacques Langevin/Sygma), 32 (David Turnley), 35 (Patrick Durand/Sygma), 36 (Bettmann); Popperfoto 11, 13 (Reuters), 23, 31 top (Reuters), 38 (Reuters), 39 top (Reuters), 41 (Reuters), 42, 43 top (Reuters), 46 (Reuters); Reuters 34 (Andrew Wong), 43 bottom (Andrew Wong); Rex Features 2–3 (Sipa), 9 (Mauro Corraro), 10 (Pacific Press), 12 (Sipa), 17 main image (Sipa), 19 (Sipa), 20 (Sipa), 24 both (Sipa), 25 bottom (Sipa), 26 (Sipa), 27 bottom (Sipa), 29 (Sipa), 30 (Sipa), 33 (Sipa), 40 (Sipa); Topham Picturepoint 8.

CONTENTS

As midnight approached on June 3, 1989, the enormous space of Tiananmen Square in China's capital, Beijing, was filled with thousands of young people. For the past two months people had been gathering in the square to protest against the rigid policies of the Chinese government. Some of the protestors were intellectuals and workers, but most were students. All were desperate to see changes in their country.

For most of April and May the atmosphere in the square had been positive. By the beginning of June the mood had changed as the government began to take serious action. On the morning of June 3 the government had given orders for the army to clear the square. Throughout the day there were shootings in the streets as Beijing citizens struggled in vain to block the progress of the tanks.

As night fell army tanks and trucks were positioned around the square. A helicopter circled above, blaring out instructions for the protestors to leave. Most of the students were huddled together around the People's Monument, ignoring all the warnings, just waiting to see what would happen next.

The students seemed calm, almost resigned. Some quietly wrote their wills. There was no sense of panic, even though the steady chatter of gunfire could be heard in the streets around the square and in the darkness beyond.

Around 2 A.M. there was an ominous rumble. Then, very slowly, the first column of transport trucks rolled into the square, edging forward at walking pace. Groups of foot soldiers dressed in riot gear and carrying rifles marched beside the trucks.

A sea of protestors fill Tiananmen Square in May 1989, when the protest was at its largest.

Gradually, as if in slow motion, hundreds of troops started pouring into the square. They spread out in all directions, firing bullets as they went. A student later reported that in the first five minutes he saw about twenty people hit by stray bullets. He said, "The soldiers were jumping for joy, as if playing a game."

Three hours later, Tiananmen Square was completely emptied of students. Hundreds of young people had been killed or wounded, mostly from gunshot wounds. Some had suffered terrible injuries and deaths, crushed under tanks. Thousands of people of all ages had been killed and injured in the streets around the square.

Within hours people around the world were reading news reports about the crackdown and watching televised images of the chaos in the streets. People everywhere reacted with horror and the students became international heroes. Even today, the effects of the Tiananmen Square crackdown are still being felt.

Chinese soldiers struggle to hold back a wave of students heading for Tiananmen Square.

Last Words

" On the night of June 3 my son let go of my hand and ran off to ride his bike to Tiananmen. This was his only hope. His classmates told us that before he died he shouted, 'Don't use force against the people.' When he was shot he said to his classmates, 'I think I may have been shot.' He thought that he had been hit by a rubber bullet. He didn't think it could have been a real bullet that pierced his heart. "

Ding Zilin, mother of Jiang Jielian, a 17-year-old high school student who was killed in Tiananmen Square

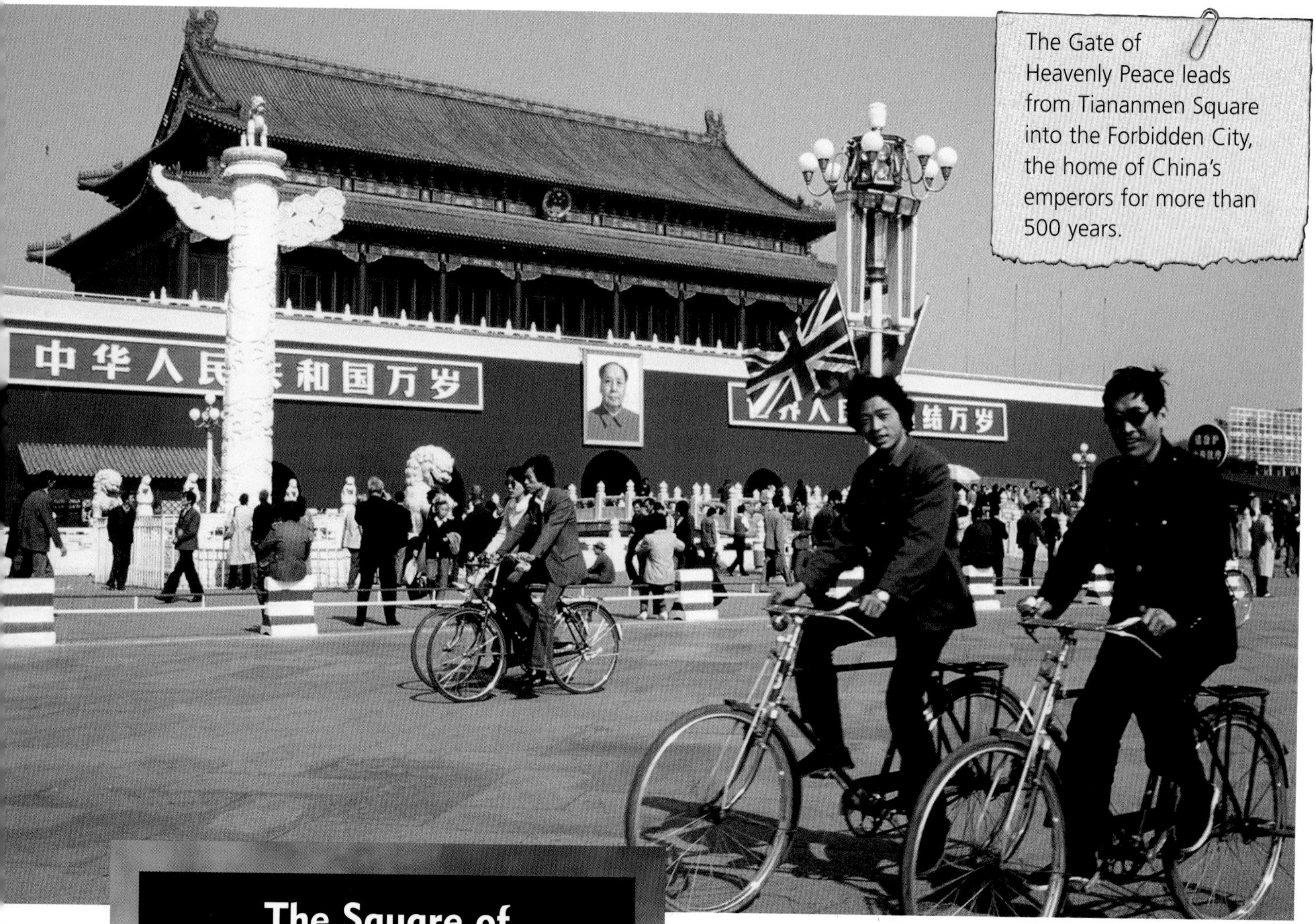

中华人民共和国万岁

全世界人民团结万岁

The Square of Heavenly Peace

Tiananmen Square was originally built in 1651 as a courtyard for the Forbidden City, the large palace of the Chinese emperors. It is named after the main gate of the palace, which stands at the northern end of the square. Tiananmen means "Gate of Heavenly Peace" in Chinese. In the 1950s the square was enlarged to four times its original size and covered in cement.

THE TIANANMEN SQUARE PROTEST WAS A reaction to the policies of the Chinese government in the 1980s. But the students' rebellion and the government's harsh response to it also had their origins in China's past. For most of its long history, China had been controlled by very powerful rulers (called emperors) while its people had remained extremely poor and powerless. China was also cut off from the rest of the world for thousands of years. It developed very differently from Western countries, and its rulers were suspicious of Western ways.

Emperors ruled over China for more than two thousand years. They made sure that their people had very little contact with "dangerous" foreigners. Qin

Shi Huangdhi, the first emperor of China, united his empire in 221 B.C.E. He set a pattern for extremely strict rule that was followed by later emperors. Anyone who disobeyed his orders was brutally punished, and books that contained ideas that contradicted those of the emperor were burned.

China's emperors lived incredibly luxurious lives in beautiful palaces. In about 1400 a large, walled palace known as the Forbidden City was built in Beijing. Only the emperor's family, advisers, and servants were allowed inside the city. Meanwhile, most people in China were extremely poor and worked as peasants in the countryside.

By the 1700s the Chinese emperors began to allow trade with Europe. But they were determined to keep foreigners out of China, so merchants were only allowed to trade at the southern port of Canton. The emperors made the merchants pay in silver for Chinese silk, tea, and porcelain. However, in the 1720s the British started paying with a drug called opium instead. The emperor was furious and banned all trade with Britain, so the British launched an attack on Chinese ports. Between 1839 and 1842 and 1856 and 1860, China and Britain fought two major wars, known as the Opium Wars, which Britain won. After the British victories, China was forced to allow British merchants to trade at many Chinese ports.

By the beginning of the 20th century, many people in China resented the power of the emperors and wanted a better life. In 1911 a group called the Kuomintang seized control of China. In the following year, the Kuomintang forced the emperor to abdicate and set up a republic in place of the empire. But not everyone supported the Kuomintang. In 1921 the Chinese Communist Party was founded. This party, which believes in sharing a country's land and profits equally among all its people, had started first in Russia in 1917. Communism soon became very popular among ordinary Chinese people, who wanted China to be run by the workers and peasants rather than by the rich.

Even after his death, China's first emperor still made his power felt. He was buried with thousands of life-sized clay warriors.

ONE GROUP OF COMMUNISTS SET UP THEIR OWN government in the south, and started to distribute land among all the people. They were supported by a large band of peasant soldiers led by an energetic young commander, Mao Tse-tung. In 1934 the communists in the south were surrounded by a Kuomintang army. Some of them managed to escape and set off on a long journey to find a safe place for their party to grow. This incredible journey covered 6,000 miles (10,000 kilometers) and is known as the Long March. Later, the story of the heroes who took part in the Long March became an important part of the history of the Chinese Communist Party (CCP).

The struggle between the CCP and the Kuomintang for control of China lasted for more than fifteen years, but eventually the communists took over the government of the country. In 1949 Mao Tse-tung announced the start of the People's Republic of China from the Gate of Heavenly Peace in Tiananmen Square.

Once he was in control, Mao set about reorganizing Chinese society, taking money and power away from the nobles and sharing the country's wealth among its people. In May 1958 Mao started a campaign known as the Great Leap Forward, which tried to build up Chinese industry very quickly. Many peasants were taken away from their farms to work in factories. This meant that not enough crops were planted and millions of people died from hunger.

During the 1960s Mao became worried that China was becoming too Westernized and that it was moving away from true communism. He was particularly concerned that teachers in schools and universities were spreading Western, capitalist ideas to their students. So he decided to concentrate on the young and, in 1966, started a campaign known as the Cultural Revolution. Mao encouraged young people to be on the lookout for Western-influenced ideas. He urged them to criticize their teachers, parents, and bosses if they showed Western sympathies and to

Mao Tse-tung leads a band of communist supporters. After many years of civil war, Mao emerged as China's first communist leader.

report them to Communist Party officials. Many schools and universities were closed, and educated people were forced to work on the land. Groups of teenagers known as the Red Guards took the law into their own hands and beat and tortured anyone they suspected of being against the principles of the Communist Party. After three years of chaos, the army was used to stop the violence, but any Western-influenced ideas were still treated with great suspicion.

Altogether, Mao ruled China for 27 years. Despite his numerous mistakes, he was greatly respected by many Chinese people because they believed he genuinely wanted to help his country. However, toward the end of his life Mao became very weak and ill, and his wife Jiang Qing took over the running of the country. Together with three politicians she formed the Gang of Four. The Gang of Four ruled China very strictly. Violent punishments were given to anyone who disagreed with their ideas. They were very unpopular among the people.

Chairman Mao waves to the crowds in Tiananmen Square. For 27 years, Mao ruled China with an iron hand.

Violence and Power

Mao was famous for his sayings, many of which were collected in a little red book called *Thoughts of Chairman Mao*. This book was distributed to everyone in China. One of Mao's most famous "thoughts" is: "All power flows from the barrel of a gun." In this saying Mao stated his belief that power has to be backed up by violence. Many members of the Chinese Communist Party also believed that it was sometimes necessary to use violence to control the people.

China's President Deng Xiaoping shakes hands with President Jimmy Carter on his historic visit to the United States in 1979.

AFTER MAO TSE-TUNG'S DEATH IN SEPTEMBER 1976, the Gang of Four remained in power. But within a month they were arrested by the army on the orders of a group of politicians led by Deng Xiaoping (see box opposite). In December 1978 Deng took total control of China as the country's Paramount (most important) Ruler.

The communist politician Deng Xiaoping was the most forward-looking leader ever to rule China. His main goals were the "four modernizations"—bringing Chinese industry, agriculture, defense, and technology up to date. He tried to move away from the rigid method of controlling the country from the center.

Instead he worked to give people more economic freedom to run their own lives. In particular, Deng encouraged farmers to run their farms as businesses, keeping the profits for themselves, instead of simply producing food for the state.

Deng took steps to end China's long isolation from the rest of the world, creating a new "open door" policy for his country. He started to hold talks with other communist countries and with the West. In 1978 Deng began negotiations with the United States government about China's place in the world. In the following year he visited the United States on the first official international trip by a senior Chinese leader.

As well as creating links with other countries, Deng made partnerships with foreign businesses, especially companies in Hong Kong, and encouraged them to build offices and hotels in China's towns and cities. Deng's policies had a dramatic effect on life in China. But while some people's lives were greatly improved, the changes also caused problems. By the late 1980s, Deng was facing criticism from many different groups of people in China.

Deng Xiaoping (1904–1997)

Deng Xiaoping joined the Communist Party as a young man and took part in the Long March. In the 1950s he became a member of the Politburo (the decision-making part of the Chinese government). But Deng did not support Mao's policies during the Cultural Revolution and was sent to be "re-educated" into true communist ways by working in a tractor factory. Deng returned to power in the 1970s and by 1974 he was Mao's right-hand man, acting as a leading minister. However, Deng's enthusiasm for more liberal policies—offering the Chinese people more freedom—made him very unpopular with the Gang of Four. In January 1976 he went into hiding for his own safety.

After Mao's death in 1976, Deng made a comeback, overthrowing the Gang of Four and taking control of China. In January 1978 at the age of 73, Deng became China's Paramount Ruler and kept this position until 1987. But even after he retired Deng remained extremely powerful behind the scenes. He was determined to turn China into a modern, forward-looking country, even if the methods he used were not always approved of by other people. He justified his actions in a famous quote: "It doesn't matter what color the cat is, so long as it catches the mouse." After the Tiananmen Square crackdown, many people remembered this saying of Deng's.

President Deng inspects his troops from his official car. Deng used the army to keep firm control of China.

During the 1980s life became especially hard for people in China's cities.

DENG XIAOPING'S CHANGES IN CHINA CREATED new opportunities for many people. In the country, farms began to prosper after years of neglect, and some farmers became rich. In cities and towns, some enterprising shopkeepers and restaurant owners began to make a profit, and people involved in the newly set up businesses made money fast. But these changes also caused a lot of problems.

As the farmers became more successful, they raised the price of food; this meant that many workers in the towns could no longer afford to buy food. In particular, people working for the government and teachers were very badly affected because their wages did not rise. All over the country, the gap between rich and poor widened, as some people profited from the changes while others suffered.

There were stories of bribery and corrupt deals between the government and its foreign business partners. Many people were suspicious of China's involvement with foreigners and thought the country was becoming dangerously "Westernized."

Under Deng's government, intellectuals (writers, teachers, and students) had very little power or status. They were also bitterly disappointed in Deng's reforms. After the Cultural Revolution came to an end they had hoped they could enjoy greater social freedom and be allowed to say what they thought and meet with whom they liked. But Deng's government kept a firm control on people's lives. The activities of intellectuals were closely watched, teachers in schools and universities were still forced to teach party slogans, and newspapers still carried the government's message. In many cases government officials continued to choose people's careers, giving them job placements, often against their wishes. This method was used especially to punish people whose ideas were threatening to the government. Students with radical ideas could be sent to work on farms in the country, far away from their friends and family.

While many people in China were growing restless, the rest of the communist world was starting to change dramatically. In 1985 Mikhail Gorbachev became leader of the Soviet Union and introduced two striking new ideas: *glasnost*—more freedom of information, free speech, and free elections—and *perestroika*—reform of the way the state was run. These ideas spread rapidly through the communist countries of Eastern Europe. In 1988 thousands of Polish workers went on strike to protest against their government. Poland's communist leaders were forced to allow democratic elections, and the workers' trade union, known as Solidarity, won a huge victory. Poland had ceased to be a communist country.

By the late 1980s a mood of rebellion was spreading like wildfire through communist Eastern Europe. People openly criticized their communist leaders and turned to Western ideas of democracy as their hope for the future. This new belief that dramatic changes were possible also spread to China. It added to the growing sense that something had to be done to make the government take notice of the people's wishes.

Calls for Democracy

During the 1980s many people in communist countries wanted a more democratic society in which individuals had the chance to control their own lives. In particular, they wanted the following:
- freedom of speech;
- freedom of the press;
- freedom of action (especially the right to choose their own jobs);
- freedom to choose their rulers in elections.

Soviet President Mikhail Gorbachev is welcomed to China in May 1989, two weeks before the crackdown in Tiananmen Square.

Although many people were unhappy with their government, it was the students who spoke out the loudest. This was not surprising in China, a country with a strong tradition of student protest. In particular, the students of Beijing University had famously made their voices heard in 1919 in a protest called the May 4 Movement (see box).

In the late 1970s Deng Xiaoping began his "four modernizations" of agriculture, industry, defense, and technology. But Chinese students and their teachers were anxious for a fifth modernization—of Chinese society. In fall 1978 students began to display posters on a stretch of wall close to the center of Beijing. The posters called on the government to make changes in society, and the wall became known as the Democracy Wall. It was used by protesters of all ages to

The May 4 Movement of 1919 led to widespread debate about China's social and political problems. The protesting students soon became national heroes.

A Moment in Time

It is early morning in Beijing on May 4, 1919, and Tiananmen Square is alive with young people waving tall banners. Thousands of students from Beijing's universities have gathered in the square to protest against the terms of the Treaty of Versailles (an agreement signed by the Western powers at the end of World War I). They feel that everyone in China should share their outrage that Chinese land previously held by Germany will be given to Japan rather than returned to China. This kind of public demonstration has never happened before in their country, and people flock to the square to hear the students' speeches. As they listen, many of them experience for the first time a new sense of patriotism (national pride).

Workers and students in Beijing study posters on the Democracy Wall.

Students gather in Shanghai as part of a nationwide protest in December 1986.

voice grievances against the government. Although the posters called for democracy, Chinese students did not want to set up a Western-style government. Almost all of them were loyal communists who hoped to reform the party by pointing out its problems.

The Democracy Wall in Beijing gave hope to many people throughout the country. By February 1979 underground magazines critical of the government were circulating in several Chinese cities. Young people gathered together in parks, where they read their poetry, played guitars, sang, and danced. The meetings had a serious political purpose—the students were demanding more freedoms—but they were also relaxed and cheerful events. But this hopeful movement was short-lived. In a tough speech in March 1979, Deng Xiaoping stated that the activities had gone too far and were interfering with China's progress on the four modernizations. Several Democracy Wall activists were arrested, and one student leader, Wei Jingsheng, was sentenced to fifteen years of hard labor.

During the early 1980s there was a series of student protests against the government, but the most extreme demonstrations took place in 1986. The year began hopefully, as Deng's government encouraged intellectuals to put forward their ideas for how society could change. But almost as soon as the debate was opened up, the supporters of social reform in the government were defeated by older and more conservative politicians who warned against dangerous Western ideas.

This harsh response unleashed a flood of protest from the students. During November and December 1986, they took to the streets in cities around China, demonstrating against the government and calling for democracy. On New Year's Day 1987, thousands of protestors gathered in Tiananmen Square, but their protest was quickly broken up by police. Deng Xiaoping announced that the young people had been led astray by troublemakers who were intent on "the total Westernization of China."

A homeless man sleeps in the streets of Beijing. During the winter of 1989, many people arrived in the cities looking for work and were forced to live on the streets and beg for food.

BY THE END OF 1988, AS DENG XIAOPING'S TEN years of reform drew to a close, China was facing a crisis situation. Farmers were not producing enough food to feed all the people, and prices were rising sharply while many people were becoming poorer. Unemployed workers from the country began to move to the towns, but there was not enough work to go around and many turned to illegal ways of making money. There was also plenty of evidence of corruption among government officials. Deng Xiaoping was old and ill (in 1988 he was 81 years old), and there were rumors that he was losing control of the Politburo.

Life was especially hard for the students. Throughout the 1980s their living conditions had been worsening.

They did not have enough food to eat and student residences were very run down. Courses were rigidly structured and there were often not enough books in the libraries. University campuses were protected by guards against so-called "hooligans" and the students' lives were very strictly controlled. For example, many students had to obey curfews and return to their homes very early in the evening. Once the students left college, the career prospects for most of them were bleak, and if they became involved in political action, they knew that they would sacrifice any hope of finding a good job.

While many people in China were becoming restless, Deng Xiaoping was quietly making preparations in case of trouble. As early as 1987 he started training

China's army—known as the People's Liberation Army (PLA)—to be ready to deal with mass riots. During the winter of 1988–1989, the PLA and the Security Bureau bought large amounts of riot control equipment, including tear gas and other crowd-controlling chemicals, clubs, and protective clothing. Selected military and security units also began training in crowd control. These specially trained units included the highly skilled 8341 military regiment, which was responsible for guarding Zhongnanhai—the headquarters of the Politburo to the west of Tiananmen Square.

In addition to making military plans, the Security Bureau purchased sets of miniature television cameras to be placed at crossroads. These tiny cameras, which had been developed by the Japanese, were smaller than a pencil sharpener. They could be automatically controlled from a central station to transmit pictures from all sides of a traffic intersection. After the Tiananmen Square incident, the government claimed that the cameras were intended for monitoring traffic offenses, but they also enabled Security Bureau staff to identify people taking part in any demonstrations.

Li Peng (1928–)

Li Peng's father was one of the first members of the Chinese Communist Party, but he was killed by the Kuomintang when Li Peng was only three. When he was eleven years old, Li Peng was adopted by the Chinese communist leader Zhou Enlai, and grew up very close to people in power. Zhou Enlai sent the young Li Peng to train as a water engineer, and in 1981 he became minister for electric power. When Deng Xiaoping retired in 1987, Li Peng was made premier (prime minister) of China. He kept this important post until 1998, when he was 70.

Although he was not one of the oldest members of the government, Li Peng joined forces with a group of older politicians, nicknamed "the elders." This group tried to slow down the pace of reform in the country and warned against "spiritual contamination"—the infection of China's youth with dangerous Western ideas. With the support of the elders, Li Peng was the driving force in suppressing the student protests. He was in charge of the country at the time of the Tiananmen Square crackdown and made sure that he hung onto power after it was over.

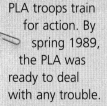

PLA troops train for action. By spring 1989, the PLA was ready to deal with any trouble.

ON APRIL 15, 1989 AN EVENT TOOK PLACE that provided a focus for the students' discontent. Hu Yaobang, the popular former party secretary, died suddenly and students throughout China went into mourning.

Hu Yaobang had been an idealistic politician who had played an important part in the social reforms in China, working hard to give people more responsibility for their own lives. In 1986 he had strongly supported the move toward greater intellectual freedom, and when the students rebelled, he refused to take action against them. This refusal led to his forced resignation in 1987. Hu had spent the last years of his life in unwilling retirement.

With Hu's death, the students lost a hero who had championed their rights. They began to gather in Tiananmen Square to commemorate Hu's life and to voice their complaints. They called for democracy, for an end to corruption among officials, and for a more open dialogue between the people and their leaders.

On April 22 an official memorial service for Hu Yaobang was held in the Great Hall of the People overlooking Tiananmen Square. Three student representatives demanded to meet Premier Li Peng. They carried a petition containing their requests for a fairer and more open society.

In front of a crowd of about 100,000 students, the representatives knelt on the steps of the Great Hall to present their petition, but the politicians completely ignored them. Greatly angered by this snub, students in many cities began to boycott (stay away from) their classes.

On April 26 the government published a message to the Chinese people through an editorial in the official newspaper, the *People's Daily*. The editorial condemned the student demonstrators, accusing a "small handful of plotters" of deliberately causing chaos. It also suggested that the government should take a firm approach to restore order and hinted that some "bloodletting" would "not be a bad thing."

In Tiananmen Square a giant portrait of Hu Yaobang is surrounded with flowers and tributes. Hu's death led to a great outburst of emotion in China.

The government's message sent a wave of anger across China. The very next day, tens of thousands of students in Beijing began to march toward Tiananmen Square to protest against the government's editorial, ignoring its warnings of a violent crackdown.

The Chinese people's reaction to the students' action was overwhelmingly positive. As the students took to the streets they were greeted enthusiastically by Beijing citizens. The police were powerless to stop the flow of people into the square. Aware of the strength of public opinion, the Chinese government did not take action against the students. Instead, government representatives agreed to hold talks with student leaders, provided that an atmosphere of calm was restored.

The promised talks were held a few days later, while the demonstrators continued their protest in the square, but the talks were not a success. The students were kept away from any top officials and felt they had been tricked. By the end of April, the students realized that they would have to find different ways to make their voices heard.

By May 4, 1989, students had taken to the streets of Beijing, defying the government's tough message published in a newspaper editorial.

Support and Encouragement

"Television pictures transmitted across the world showed workers rushing out of their factories to greet the students, offering snacks and drinks or just a hand raised in support. 'We love the students!' onlookers shouted. 'We love the people!' was the reply."

An account of the student march of April 27, 1989, from Ruth Cherrington's China's Students: The Struggle for Democracy

On May 4, 1989, dancing students celebrate the 70th anniversary of the student protests of May 1919.

THE MONTH OF MAY 1989 CONTAINED TWO very important dates. The first was May 4, the 70th anniversary of the famous student protest in Tiananmen Square at the end of World War I (see page 16). The second was May 17, when President Mikhail Gorbachev of Russia was scheduled to visit China for talks with the Chinese government for the first time in more than 30 years.

On May 4, 1989, about 60,000 students held a lively demonstration in Tiananmen Square with speeches, singing, and dancing. The students were joined by workers and journalists demanding fairer working conditions and freedom of the press. Crowds lined the streets around the square, cheering them on.

On the same day, Party Secretary Zhao Ziyang gave some surprising signs of support for the student movement. In a speech to international members of the Asian Development Bank, Zhao did not condemn the student protests and even acknowledged that some of their demands were "reasonable." Zhao was well known for his liberal views. His speech was welcomed by the students as a hopeful sign.

The week following May 4 was relatively quiet, but as the visit of President Gorbachev approached the students decided to take a more dramatic stand. On May 13 thousands of students marched to Tiananmen Square, and several hundred of them announced they were going on hunger strike. They stated that they would refuse all food and stay in the square until the government agreed to a genuine conversation with them.

News of the hunger strike brought crowds of sympathizers to the square. They were deeply touched by the young people's sacrifice. The emotional scenes were recorded by photographers and journalists from all over the world, who were already in China to report on Gorbachev's visit.

Party Secretary Zhao Ziyang visits a hunger striker in the hospital. Zhao Ziyang was the only member of the Chinese government to show sympathy for the students.

By the time Gorbachev arrived in China, the government was in a very difficult position. More than 3,000 students had joined the hunger strike, and the government faced the prospect of being held responsible for a large number of young deaths. A planned ceremony in Tiananmen Square was cancelled and the Russian visitors were kept away from the square as much as possible. But it was impossible to ignore the crowds that had gathered there, and the wail of ambulance sirens as collapsing hunger strikers were rushed to the hospital.

On May 18 Premier Li Peng and Zhao Ziyang visited some of the hunger strikers in the hospital and agreed to hold talks with them. Later that day the students arrived at the Great Hall of the People looking exhausted—one was still wearing his pajamas and carrying an intravenous drip! However, no progress was made. Li Peng remained proud and aloof, and in the end the students walked out in disgust.

The Patriotic Democratic Movement

The Chinese student protest movement of the late 1980s is often known as the Patriotic Democratic Movement. This name reflects the two different aspects of the students' cause. The students campaigned for a more open, democratic society with greater freedom for the Chinese people (see page 15). But they were also patriotic—intensely proud of their country and its history. Almost all the students still thought of themselves as communists and did not want China to become a Westernized, capitalist country.

ON MAY 18 PRESIDENT GORBACHEV LEFT China. Although the Chinese and Russian leaders had begun to discuss restoring good relations between their countries, it was clear that their talks had been seriously affected by the student action. So, the following morning, Premier Li Peng was in a grim mood when he and Party Secretary Zhao Ziyang visited Tiananmen Square at dawn. Li Peng seemed unmoved by the sight of so many weakened young people and told the students briskly that they should go home. But the more liberal Zhao Ziyang was clearly upset. In a heartfelt and emotional speech he apologized to the students, saying: "I have come too late."

Later on in the day, more than a million people took to the streets of Beijing to demonstrate against the government, chanting "Save the children! Save the nation!" The city was plunged into chaos and most people stayed away from work. Meanwhile, in the square the students held a vote on whether to continue the hunger strike. Many of the hunger strikers were now dangerously ill and the students were afraid of what the government might do next. They voted by a narrow margin to call off the hunger strike but to continue occupying the square.

In the early hours of Saturday May 20, at a special meeting of the Communist Party congress, a grim-faced Li Peng declared martial law (control by the army) in parts of Beijing. He spoke of the "turmoil" and "chaos" caused by the students and of the threat they posed to the security of the country. Li Peng was backed by the elders, including some party officials who were so old they had to be brought in wheelchairs. But the moderate Party Secretary Zhao Ziyang was nowhere to be seen. Clearly, the hardliners had taken control of the government.

A solitary protester with a rose faces a row of guards in Tiananmen Square.

"I have no voice." A student wears a gag to show he has been silenced by the Chinese government.

Li Peng set a deadline of 5 A.M. the following morning for the square to be cleared, after which the army would move in. But the students refused to be frightened away. Some groups drifted off but thousands stayed, apparently ready to sacrifice their lives for their principles. To keep their spirits up, they repeatedly sang the "Internationale" (the song of the communist movement) and the Chinese national anthem.

Meanwhile, PLA troops waiting on the outskirts of Beijing began to move slowly toward the center of the city. But before they could make much progress, a squad of young motorcyclists known as the Flying Tigers warned the people of Beijing that the army was coming. All over the city, groups of residents rushed out to set up roadblocks, using things like buses, trucks, and dumpsters to block the soldiers' path.

Once the soldiers were no longer able to move, the people started to reason with them, begging them not to hurt the students. Most of the PLA soldiers had no idea what was happening in the city and were easily won over. Only a few scuffles were reported as the army was peacefully stopped in its tracks. Li Peng's attempt to enforce martial law had been foiled by a remarkable show of "people power."

A Beijing policeman offers a gesture of support to students on their way to the square.

A bus is dragged across a street to prevent troops from advancing further into the city.

Protecting the Students

❝We all had the same mind, the same idea. No one told us what to do. We just went out on the streets to stop the army. The Party no longer controlled us.... We all went out to protect the students.❞

An elderly woman involved in holding back the army in Beijing in May 1989

PREMIER LI PENG'S ANNOUNCEMENT OF MARTIAL law on May 20 set off a wave of demonstrations in cities all over China. Meanwhile, on the streets of Beijing there was a new mood of defiance following the successful holding back of the troops. People expressed their support for the students by singing, dancing, and chanting slogans. By May 23 all the troops had retreated to the outskirts of Beijing.

However, in spite of the widespread demonstrations a sense of stalemate soon began to set in. The government was clearly not responding to demands, and it had withdrawn once more into unreachable silence. The next meeting of the government congress was not scheduled until June 20.

By the last week in May, the strain on the student protestors was beginning to show. Many began to leave the square and there were problems finding enough food for those that remained. The students

made determined efforts to organize themselves, forming a committee to coordinate their efforts and establishing a "Defend Tiananmen Square" headquarters. On May 27 the committee recommended that the occupation of the square should end by May 30. However, at the last minute a group of radical students took over and made a new resolution. They would stay in the square until June 20, the date for the next meeting of the government congress.

Despite their determination to continue, the students were desperately in need of a new source of inspiration, and they found it in the shape of a Styrofoam statue. During the night of May 29 the 33-foot (10-meter) high statue was wheeled into Tiananmen Square, supported on six bicycles. The statue was the work of students at the Central Academy of Fine Arts. It closely resembled the Statue of Liberty, and was intended to represent the spirit of freedom and democracy.

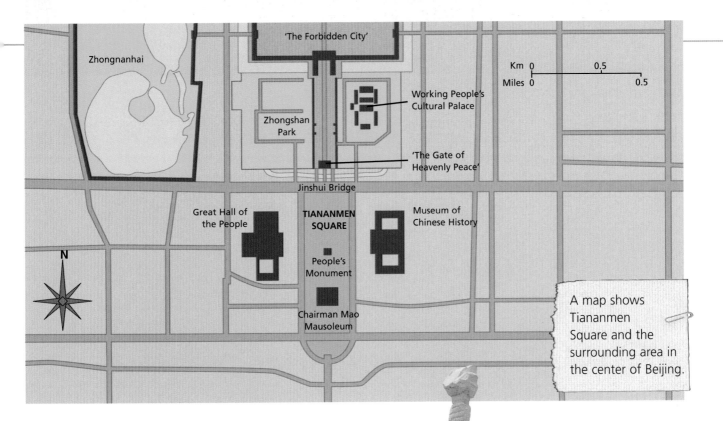

Zhongnanhai

Working People's Cultural Palace

Zhongshan Park

'The Gate of Heavenly Peace'

Jinshui Bridge

Km 0   0.5
Miles 0   0.5

Great Hall of the People

TIANANMEN SQUARE

Museum of Chinese History

People's Monument

N

Chairman Mao Mausoleum

A map shows Tiananmen Square and the surrounding area in the center of Beijing.

In a deliberate act of defiance, the glaringly bright, white statue was placed opposite the huge portrait of Chairman Mao. The "Goddess of Liberty" was unveiled in a solemn ceremony in front of members of the international press. It immediately became a gathering point for the students and a symbol of their struggle and their ideals. One student said: "Soldiers will try to knock it down, but not yet. We must protect the statue!"

The large Styrofoam statue of the Goddess of Liberty is surrounded by students and members of the press.

Nonviolent Struggle

At the beginning of June, the student protesters were visited by Dr. Gene Sharp, an American academic from Harvard University. Dr. Sharp, who specializes in the study of nonviolent struggle, observed that the students used entirely peaceful methods of protest and resistance. He concluded that they had worked out their nonviolent strategy themselves, rather than learning about it from books. But they did have some knowledge of the nonviolent methods used by Mahatma Gandhi in India and the Solidarity movement in Poland.

By early June many of the students were close to collapse. The square was constantly filled with noise and activity so it was very hard to sleep. Most of the protestors were also suffering from lack of proper food. They had survived for weeks on whatever the citizens could spare—mainly noodles and water—and were now very weak. Everyone in the square was in a constant state of alert, waiting for the sound of approaching troops.

At 5 P.M. on Friday, June 2, a new hunger strike was announced. It was to be on a much smaller scale than before, but would involve a number of well-known figures. One of the hunger strikers, Hou Dejian, was a rock star who had been inspired by the students' cause. The presence of Hou Dejian, who came from Taiwan—a country that had broken away from communist China in 1949—acted as a magnet for the city's young people. All through the evening of June 2, students kept pouring into the square on their bicycles.

Meanwhile, in other parts of the city PLA troops were clearly visible, preparing to move as soon as they were given the order. There were rumors that soldiers were trying to get on friendly terms with Beijing citizens, but the people remained determined in their support of the students.

On the night of June 2, two companies of soldiers starting marching toward Tiananmen Square, but neither of them reached the center. One group was surrounded by citizens and prevented from moving forward. The other group, accompanied by buses and tanks, was involved in a traffic accident in which two citizens were killed. Surrounded by angry crowds, the soldiers eventually turned back.

Students settle down for the night in Tiananmen Square. Some protestors had tents, but many slept in the open on the ground.

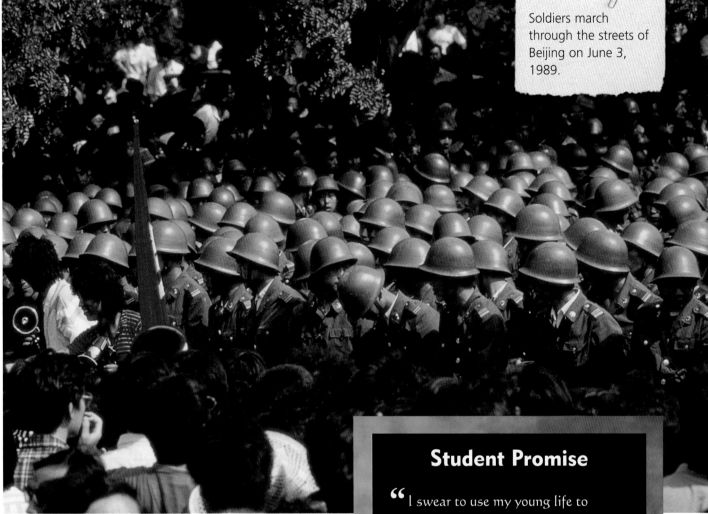

Soldiers march through the streets of Beijing on June 3, 1989.

Student Promise

"I swear to use my young life to protect the square. Our heads may be cut off, our blood may flow, but the People's Square must not be lost."

An oath sworn by students in Tiananmen Square on June 3, 1989

By the morning of June 3, soldiers were taking up positions close to the square, although some were still held back by barricades erected by angry citizens in the streets. During the afternoon a series of violent clashes took place between the soldiers and Beijing citizens, the people shouting and throwing stones, while the soldiers shot to kill.

By the evening of June 3, PLA troops had broken through all the barricades and surrounded the square. The city was filled with burning vehicles. Hundreds of citizens were killed in the struggle to hold back the troops. Some were crushed by tanks and armored personnel carriers, and others were shot at point-blank range.

The Chinese government broadcast a message saying: "Counter-revolutionary rebellion is now taking place. Ruffians are violently attacking PLA soldiers.... They [intend] to overthrow the People's Republic of China." Clearly the government was prepared to take any measures needed to crush the protest. The outlook for the students in the square looked grim.

Tanks roll into Tiananmen Square in the early hours of June 4.

BY MIDNIGHT ON JUNE 3 MOST OF THE STUDENTS had withdrawn to the People's Monument in the southeast of the square where they sat, huddled together, wondering what the next day would bring. They did not have long to wait.

1:00 A.M. People who had witnessed the killing of civilians on the streets of Beijing reported to the students' command headquarters, urging them to leave the square. But student commander-in-chief, Chai Ling, appealed to the protestors to stay.

2:00 A.M. The first column of troop transport trucks rolled into the square, moving slowly forward. Accompanying the trucks were groups of foot soldiers wearing steel helmets and carrying assault rifles. The soldiers fanned out slowly along the northern edge of the square and sealed off the northeast entrance. Some students were shot as the soldiers pressed forward.

3:00 A.M. Thousands of silent soldiers, each armed with a rifle and a long wooden cudgel, positioned themselves around the square. Only a small exit corridor in the southeast was left open.

With the protesters torn between staying and leaving, two of the hunger strikers—the rock star, Hou Dejian, and the economist, Zhou Duo—began to negotiate with army officials to give the students time to leave the square safely. The officials stressed that withdrawal had to be unconditional (in other words, the protestors could not make any demands) and the square had to be emptied by daybreak.

4:00 A.M. Suddenly, all the lights went off in the square and the statue of the Goddess of Liberty was toppled by a tank. For fifteen minutes there was nothing but darkness and silence. The students remained on the Monument, and no one made a move to leave.

4:15 A.M. The square was flooded with light again, and the southernmost doors of the Great Hall swung open, releasing a stream of armed troops. These soldiers formed an L-shaped line in front of the Mao Mausoleum and fired warning shots at the Monument.

4:30 A.M. A member of the workers' union (see box) warned the protesters: "We must leave here immediately, a terrible bloodbath is about to take place." The student leaders organized a vote, and the students eventually agreed to leave. Led by Chai Ling and Feng Congde, they began to walk away from the Monument toward the southeast corner of the square.

5:00 A.M. As the students began to leave the square, a row of armored vehicles moved slowly toward the Monument. Other troops moved in from the west, pushing the crowd together and flattening the student tents. Soldiers followed the students toward the exit, firing shots in the air. Hundreds of protesters were injured and about 300 were killed.

By 7 A.M. on the morning of Sunday June 4, Tiananmen Square had been emptied and the protest was over.

Labor Union

Mingling with the students on the night of June 3 was a small but determined group of protestors known as the BWAF—the Beijing Workers Autonomous Federation. This powerful labor union campaigned fiercely for workers' rights and many of its members were prepared to use violence to achieve their ends. Many experts think that Deng's government saw the BWAF rather than the students as the real threat in the square (see page 40).

Supported by his friends, a wounded protester holds up a soldier's helmet.

Dead civilians lie among mangled bicycles near Tiananmen Square on the morning of June 4.

Sunday, June 4 dawned on a city in chaos. The streets were full of mangled metal and broken glass—the remains of the barricades put up to stop the army's progress. A number of roads remained blocked, and upturned buses and trucks, many of them still burning, littered the city. Dead bodies lay on the streets around Tiananmen Square, and wounded students were being rushed to the hospital in any vehicles that could be found, such as carts, rickshaws, and buses.

The people of Beijing wandered through their city in a daze, unable to believe what had happened. Students searched desperately for their lost companions, while some angry citizens attacked the police and soldiers. Occasional bursts of gunfire could still be heard as soldiers fired at unruly citizens. Meanwhile, Tiananmen Square was a sea of green army uniforms, as the soldiers removed all traces of the student occupation, burning their tents and possessions in large bonfires.

For five days following the crackdown nothing was heard of Deng Xiaoping and rumors began to circulate that he was ill or even dead. Eventually, on June 9, Deng appeared on television looking very old and shaky. In his speech to the people Deng announced that the government had suppressed a "counter-

Aftermath

❝ I looked over at Tiananmen and wondered how it could have been cleared so quickly.… Thick black smoke rose from the spot where the 'Goddess' had stood.… Beyond the square in all directions were clouds of smoke and the sound of shooting. It seemed as if the whole city was being destroyed. ❞

A Western observer describes the scene in Beijing in the early morning of June 4, 1989

Wrecked and burned-out vehicles litter the streets around Tiananmen Square.

revolutionary rebellion" in which the "dregs of society" had tried to "establish a bourgeois republic dependent entirely on the West."

The government worked hard to spread its version of events through television broadcasts and newspapers. Officials stated that the square had been cleared peacefully with no loss of life and that the only killings had been of "thugs" who had attempted to stop the army from carrying out its duty. There were pictures of soldiers cleaning up the city, and the troops were praised for their bravery and efficiency. The government also published pictures of leading protesters who had been arrested, looking defeated and humiliated.

After about a week, life in Beijing began to return to normal, although everyone had been changed by the crackdown. Citizens were frightened into silence as the government started to arrest activists, sympathizers, and "rumor-mongers." As a result, people simply stopped talking about the part they had played in the events in and around Tiananmen Square. Gradually all the workers who had gone out on strike in support of the students drifted back to their jobs, afraid of punishment if they stayed away. The students were in mourning for their lost companions, and the atmosphere in the universities was demoralized and cautious. Everyone knew that they were being observed by government agents who were on the lookout for any signs of rebellion.

Student leaders are arrested and led away by police officers.

Police watch a peaceful pro-democracy protest in southern China in May 1989. This was part of a massive wave of protests that took place all over China that year.

ALTHOUGH THE CITY OF BEIJING WAS THE CENTER of the protests in 1989, the pro-democracy movement spread far beyond the capital. During the 1980s people all over China had become critical of the government and, by spring 1989, there were demonstrations in cities and towns throughout the country.

The student demonstrations of the 1980s followed the same pattern all over China. Before 1989 there had been occasional protests, mainly about poor living conditions, but these were generally not very large or well organized. However, the death of Party Secretary Hu Yaobang on April 15 (see page 20) provided a focus for the students' discontent. Throughout the country, students held demonstrations to celebrate the life of "a warrior for the people's cause" and to call on the government to make China more democratic.

The next important trigger for protests across the country was Li Peng's declaration of martial law on May 20. This resulted in mass demonstrations involving workers as well as students. Some students set up barricades in the streets, and broadcast antigovernment speeches.

Finally, the Tiananmen Square crackdown of June 4, 1989, unleashed the biggest protests of all. Massive marches were organized throughout China, as people surged through city centers, some marching and waving banners, and others driving trucks plastered with posters.

Although most of the protests in the provinces were nonviolent, there were some clashes between protesters and local police. The most famous of these took place in the city of Xi'an, and became known as the April 22 incident. Here, marching students were joined by groups of unemployed young men, and the demonstration soon got out of hand. The gatehouse to the government headquarters was set on fire and the fire department was called. When the firefighters turned their hoses on the protesters, a riot developed, and police started charging the crowd, beating the demonstrators with sticks and clubs. Old people, women, and children were injured and some shops were wrecked. Witnesses saw police dragging some protesters behind police lines and beating them severely.

The April 22 incident was probably one of the reasons for the harsh government message in the *People's Daily* of April 26, in which "hooligans" were blamed for creating "turmoil and chaos" in China (see page 20).

Despite all the anger unleashed throughout the country in June 1989, the mood of defiance did not last. After the initial reaction to the crackdown had subsided, people across China became demoralized and ceased to protest in public. As in Beijing, students and workers were afraid of the prospect of arrest and discouraged by the lack of any government response. The country settled down again to an uneasy peace.

A Moment in Time

On the morning of May 19, 1989, a demonstration is turning violent in the streets of Shaoyang City. Someone has set a car on fire and it is burning fiercely. Among the crowd watching the demonstration is a fifteen-year-old school student, Liu Xin, who has been taken along by his brother-in-law to see what is happening in his city. Suddenly, Liu Xin is arrested by the police and charged with supplying matches to the demonstrators. Liu Xin protests that he is innocent and says he does not have anything to do with the demonstrators, but it is no use. He is taken off to prison.

(Liu Xin is scheduled to be released in June 2004, at the age of 30, after having spent half his life in prison.)

Army tanks move in to break up a demonstration in Beijing on June 8. After the Tiananmen crackdown, the Chinese government began to use harsher methods to put a stop to protests.

NEWS OF THE CRACKDOWN IN TIANANMEN Square soon reached the rest of the world. Television and newspaper reports were full of images of tanks bearing down on defenseless young people. The news agencies announced that thousands of students had been killed on the night of June 4. In reality, the crackdown left hundreds rather than thousands dead in the square, but the shocking fact remained that armed soldiers and tanks had been used to break up a nonviolent student demonstration. People everywhere were horrified.

In the days following the Tiananmen crackdown, government leaders all over the world spoke out against the Chinese government's actions. United States President George Bush imposed an immediate ban on all military sales to China. He also put a stop to any planned visits by Chinese or American military leaders to each others' countries.

All Change

“During the years 1978 to 1989 China managed to create an image (however inaccurate) as the more human face of communism… [But] the Tiananmen 'crackdown' of June 1989 obliterated newly formed images of China. Particularly in the West there was horror, outrage, revulsion…. The lenses through which China had previously been perceived needed to be refocused.”

From China in the 1990s *by Robert Benewick and Paul Wingrove*

Images like this one of a lone Chinese student facing a row of tanks were seen on televisions all over the world and caused widespread horror.

U.S. President George Bush took a tough line against China. He is shown here announcing a ban on U.S. military sales to China.

Within a few months, most of the links with foreign countries that Deng Xiaoping had worked so hard to create had been broken. The five years leading to 1989 had seen great progress in Chinese foreign relations as Deng developed his "open door" policy. In particular, China had developed strong ties with the United States and was working toward a major agreement with the Soviet Union. During the late 1980s, the United States, Japan, and the countries of the European Community (EC) had begun a system of "exchange visits" between high-level military, cultural, and economic staff and their corresponding officials in China.

By 1988 China belonged to to the World Bank and the International Monetary Fund (IMF), each of which were lending China large sums of money to spend on economic development. China was also applying to become a member of GATT (General Agreement on Tariffs and Trade)—an international organization that encouraged free trade between countries.

However, after the crackdown, China's famous "open door" was banged firmly shut. Within two weeks,

President Bush had suspended all senior staff exchanges with China, and the European Community and Japan soon followed America's lead. The World Bank put a stop to all lending to China, the IMF postponed work on all technical projects, and the negotiations on China's entry into GATT were suspended.

China received some support after the crackdown from the communist governments of Eastern Europe, who praised the Chinese authorities' firm and decisive action. In particular, the extreme left-wing government of East Germany congratulated the Deng administration on its suppression of a "counter-revolutionary rebellion."

However, by spring 1989 people throughout Eastern Europe were reacting against their rigid communist leaders (see page 40), and a powerful wave of sympathy for the Chinese students swept through most of the communist world. Many expert commentators believe that the crackdown in Tiananmen Square helped to encourage the rebellions in Eastern Europe. These uprisings brought down most of the communist leaders there in the second half of 1989.

China's President Jiang Zemin and U.S. President Bill Clinton wave to reporters during Jiang's visit to Washington, D.C., in 1997.

AFTER THE PROTESTS, THE MOST OBVIOUS CHANGE in China was a tightening of government control. The protest leaders were swiftly rounded up and sent to prison, while many people who had been involved in the demonstrations were given job placements in isolated parts of China. In October 1989 a law controlling mass rallies and demonstrations was passed, and martial law was not lifted in Beijing until January 1990.

The protests did not result in any radical changes in the Chinese government. If anything, the government became more conservative. It continued to be dominated by the elders, led by Premier Li Peng, while Party Secretary Zhao Ziyang, who had spoken out in favor of the students, was immediately replaced by a more committed communist, Jiang Zemin. Jiang had been mayor of Shanghai in the late 1980s and was responsible for the relatively peaceful suppression of student demonstrations there in 1989.

Deng Xiaoping retired from politics in November 1989 but remained a powerful influence in China. At the age of 88, he was still touring the country, campaigning for economic reforms. In 1997, six months after his death, Deng's ideas were made part of China's official ideology.

Jiang Zemin became China's president in 1993. He continued Deng's policy of modernizing China, creating an economy in which businesses could thrive. Under Jiang, China moved steadily toward a more Western-style market economy, and most people in China became better off. In 1997 the Chinese took over Hong Kong, a former British colony on the coast of southern China. They continued to run it as a thriving commercial and business center.

However, China's progress toward modernization has not been accompanied by an increase in democratic freedoms. Long prison sentences are still handed out to anyone who dares to criticize the authorities. China is no closer to holding elections and there is very little freedom of speech or freedom of press.

Following the world's reaction to the Tiananmen crackdown, the Chinese government became deeply suspicious of foreign countries, especially those in the West. It feared that foreign nations would try to interfere in the way that China was governed and turn the Chinese people against their government. Recently, however, China has begun to restore links with its old foreign partners and is now involved in many international organizations. It has a very important global role to play. The sixth-largest trading nation in the world, China contains one-fifth of the world's population and possesses nuclear weapons. During the past ten years many foreign leaders have visited China, and some have taken the opportunity to speak out on its government's poor record on human rights.

President Clinton and his family stroll along the Great Wall of China in 1998. While he was in China, Clinton took the opportunity to raise questions about the government's record on human rights.

A New Era

" China still faces enormous difficulties, some of them of its own making: pollution, urban sprawl ... the continuing risks of political authoritarianism.... But now ... as we look forward to the new millennium, we see a China which has overcome formidable obstacles, which has gone from being the 'sick man of Asia' to being one of the world's largest and fastest developing economies. "

From China in the 1990s *by Robert Benewick and Paul Wingrove*

Many of China's cities, such as Shanghai, are now thriving commercial centers.

WHAT MIGHT HAVE HAPPENED IN CHINA IF the Tiananmen crackdown had not taken place? One possibility is that the mood of protest set in motion by the student demonstrations could have become so powerful that it swept through the whole of China, involving not only students but also organized groups of workers. Despite the Chinese government's rigid control, there could have come a moment when the power of the people was just too strong for the authorities to resist. The communist government might have collapsed and elections might have been held for a new, democratic administration.

This is exactly what happened in the communist countries of Eastern Europe at the end of the 1980s. In one country after another, a powerful people's rebellion led to the fall of the communist government and its replacement by a new, democratic system.

Most of these revolts happened in the second half of 1989, after the Tiananmen crackdown, but one major uprising had already taken place in Poland in 1988. There, the powerful and well-organized workers' trade union known as Solidarity organized a mass strike that brought down the government. It was a stunning example of the power of the workers when they are organized into unions.

The Chinese government was well aware of the threat from labor unions, and many expert commentators say that it was not the students but the unions that the government was really intent on crushing in 1989.

In Poland, Solidarity members and their supporters gather to protest against the communist government. Their action led to the Polish government's downfall in 1988.

Crackdown or Chaos?

" If the way we handled the Tiananmen crisis was incorrect, we would not have today's prosperity. China would be in chaos. The people would have risen and resisted the government. "

Zhu Muzhi, President of the China Society for Human Rights Studies (an organization that advises the Chinese government), speaking in 2002

When the government put on a show of force to clear the square of the students, some believe they were really issuing a much more serious threat to the unions. In the words of an old Chinese proverb, they were "killing the chickens to catch the monkey."

The Tiananmen crackdown could therefore be seen as a clever move on the part of the Chinese government. It frightened off a defenseless group of unarmed students instead of confronting its real enemy, the labor unions. While the students could be overcome with a minimum of bloodshed, a confrontation with the workers would have been a much more violent affair. This is how the Chinese government has justified its actions.

Another possible outcome of the Tiananmen Square protests could have been that the Chinese government might have listened to the students' demands and begun to make changes in the way China was run. People might have had more right to speak out, the press might have been given more freedom, and elections might have been slowly introduced. However, the Chinese government feared that these measures would unleash a flood of protest and unrest and that as a result China would collapse into chaos. Jiang's government claimed it would not have been able to make progress in modernizing China if the country had been in chaos.

Supporters of the Chinese government say that its method of introducing modernization without social freedom has allowed the country to make stunning economic progress. They point to the example of the former Soviet Union, where democratic freedoms were introduced in the early 1990s, but where the economy is in ruins.

People wait in line for milk in Moscow in 1998. Although Russia has moved toward democracy, many of its people have had to face poverty.

Not Forgotten

"A decade has gone by, but the victims of 1989 are not forgotten. As long as these injustices continue, victims' relatives and campaigners worldwide will keep calling for them to end."

From a statement issued by the international human rights campaign group, Amnesty International, on the tenth anniversary of the Tiananmen Square crackdown

TODAY, PEOPLE IN CHINA RARELY TALK ABOUT THE events of 1989. This is partly the result of the government's determined efforts to suppress all mention of the crackdown, but it is also because the majority of people feel that China has moved on. Most Chinese people see their standard of living rising steadily, and although they realize they have fewer freedoms than the people of other countries, they do not think it worth risking their jobs and security by protesting against the government.

Even today, the Chinese government still keeps a tight control on any discussion of the student protests. Despite repeated appeals from pressure groups inside China and abroad, the government has refused to publish any account of the numbers of people killed, injured, or imprisoned in 1989, or to offer any compensation to the victims' families. There are still at least 200 protestors who were taken prisoner in

1989 and have never been released. Those who have been let out of prison have had their movements closely monitored and their freedom restricted. Meanwhile, the number of victims continues to increase, as people in China who campaign for a review of the 1989 events are arrested for drawing attention to the Tiananmen crackdown.

Women soldiers march through Tiananmen Square as part of a massive parade to celebrate the fiftieth anniversary of the communist People's Republic of China. The Chinese are proud of their history and their self-discipline.

In 2001 a set of official government documents on the events of June 1989 was published in a book called *The Tiananmen Papers*. The papers were compiled by Zhang Liang, a member of the Jiang government who left China to live in the United States. They contain many official records of the events of June 1989.

The book, which was edited by two U.S. authors, has sold thousands of copies in the West. It has helped people to reassess exactly what happened in the square by revealing many facts that were previously unknown. However, in China the news of the publication of *The Tiananmen Papers* led to a new round of arrests. Twenty people were detained by the police on suspicion of smuggling documents out of the country.

Recently there have been a few hopeful signs that the Chinese government's attitude toward peaceful protests may be starting to change. In his *Government Work Report of 1999*, Prime Minister Zhu Rongji instructed troops dealing with protests not to use "dictatorial means against the people." This was a direct warning against the violent treatment of

Problems continue in Tiananmen Square. Policemen arrest a member of a banned protest movement on New Year's Day, 2001.

protesters. Meanwhile, another member of the Politburo told the army to listen to public complaints and be patient in its dealings with public discontent.

Zhang Liang says he is confident that the younger wing of the Chinese Communist Party will slowly start to liberalize China. He also believes that the next generation of Chinese leaders will announce a change of attitude toward the student movement of the 1980s. If this change really comes about, the Tiananmen Square protest will not have been entirely in vain.

Glossary

abdicate to give up a position of power

activist someone who takes action to make things change

Asian Development Bank bank that lends money to help countries in Asia

assault rifle type of gun used to attack large groups of people

bourgeois interested in material things, and in becoming rich

bribery offer of money or a gift in return for doing something

capitalism economic system in which all the land, houses, factories, etc., belong to private individuals rather than to the state

CCP the Chinese Communist Party

commemorate to do something special to remember a person or an event

communism political and economic system in which the land, houses, factories, etc., belong to the state, and the profits are shared among everyone

communist someone who believes in communism

congress large meeting (as in Communist Party congress)

conservative cautious, eager to keep things as they are

counter-revolutionary against the revolution. The Chinese government used this term to suggest that the student activities were against the spirit of the original communist revolution.

crackdown strong action intended to stop something from happening

cudgel thick stick used for beating someone

democracy system of government in which the people choose their leaders in elections

detain to keep a person in prison

dialogue two-way discussion

editorial (as in newspaper editorial) written comments on events in the news.

elders name given to a group of mostly older Chinese politicians who were very powerful in the 1980s and 1990s

European Community (EC) group of countries in Europe that had special trade and political agreements with each other. The EC has now been renamed the EU (European Union).

GATT (General Agreement on Tariffs and Trade) international organization that encourages trade between nations

hard labor very hard, physical work

hardliner someone with strong beliefs who is not moderate and will not change his or her mind

human rights right of all people to have justice, fair treatment, and free speech

ideology set of ideas that someone believes in

intellectuals people who think hard about the world and share their ideas with others through discussion and writing

International Monetary Fund (IMF) international organization set up to encourage trade between nations

intravenous drip bag containing blood or some other fluid that is slowly pumped through a tube into a patient's body

Kuomintang Chinese political party founded in 1911 that overthrew the emperor. The Kuomintang is now the ruling party in Taiwan.

job placement work that is assigned to someone

labor (trade) union organized group of workers, set up to improve working conditions and pay

left-wing in favor of workers' rights and the equal sharing of wealth

liberal generally accepting of new ideas and change

market economy way of running a country that is led by what people want to buy

martial law control of a country by the army

paramount most important

party secretary very important position in the Chinese government. The party secretary is the leader of the government but is under the control of the paramount ruler.

peasant someone who works on the land. Peasants are usually very poor.

petition written request for something, usually signed by many people

PLA the People's Liberation Army, the army of the Chinese government

point-blank very close range

Politburo the decision-making part of the Chinese government

radical extreme beliefs

rallies large meetings

republic country or state that does not have a king, queen, or other absolute ruler

rickshaw two-wheeled passenger vehicle pulled by one or two men

Security Bureau department of the Chinese government that is responsible for keeping the country peaceful

slogans short, catchy messages intended to communicate an idea

social reform changes in the way a country is run

stalemate position in an argument or conflict in which both sides are stuck, and neither can make a move

status someone's position in society

Styrofoam type of molded, very light plastic

underground (as in magazines/pamphlets) published and spread secretly

World Bank international organization set up to help developing nations, usually by providing loans

Further Reading

Allan, Tony. *The Long March: The Making of Communist China*. Chicago: Heinemann, 2001.

Allan, Tony. *The Rise of Modern China*. Chicago: Heinemann, 2002.

Barth, Kelly (ed.). *The Tiananmen Square Massacre*. Farmington Hills, Mich.: Gale Group, 2003.

Liang, Zhang, Perry Link, and Andrew J. Nathan. *The Tiananmen Papers: The Chinese Leadership's Decision to Use Force Against Their Own People—In Their Own Words*. New York: PublicAffairs, 2002.

Films

The Gate of Heavenly Peace, produced by Richard Gordon and Carma Hinton, PBS, 1994. This documentary film has an excellent website at http://www.tsquare.tv, which includes information on the making of the film, a tour of Tiananmen Square, a discussion of the themes of the film, and a reading list.

Timeline

221 B.C.E. Qin Shi Huangdhi, the first emperor of China, unites China and starts a tradition of very strict rule.

c.1400 C.E. The Ming emperors begin to build the Forbidden City in Beijing.

1800s The Chinese government fights European traders for control of Chinese trade.

1911 The Kuomintang starts a revolution in China.

1912 The last emperor of China abdicates.

1919 May 4 Movement takes place, a student protest in Tiananmen Square against the terms of the Treaty of Versailles made at the end of the First World War.

1920 The Communist Party is founded.

1934 The Long March, led by Mao Tse-tung, prevents the Communist Party from being wiped out.

1949 Mao Tse-tung announces the start of the People's Republic of China in Tiananmen Square. Mao starts the Great Leap Forward, which leads to the death of millions from hunger. Mao starts the Cultural Revolution.

1976 Mao Tse-tung dies and the Gang of Four are arrested.

Autumn 1978 Students set up a Democracy Wall in Beijing.

December 1978 Deng Xiaoping takes control of China. He soon begins his "four modernizations."

1985 Mikhail Gorbachev becomes leader of the Soviet Union and begins to introduce social reforms.

November 1986 Student demonstrations take place against the government in many Chinese cities.

January 1987 Deng's government cracks down on the student protests.

April 15, 1989 Death of Hu Yaobang, the former party secretary, leads to an outbreak of protests.

April 22, 1989 Three student representatives present a petition to Premier Li Peng. On the same day there are violent demonstrations in the city of Xi'an.

April 26, 1989 Government editorial in the *People's Daily* condemning the student demonstrators.

May 4, 1989 Student demonstration in Tiananmen Square marks the anniversary of the May 4 Movement.

May 13, 1989 Hundreds of students in Tiananmen Square announce a hunger strike.

May 17, 1989 President Gorbachev arrives in Beijing for talks with the Chinese government.

May 20, 1989 Premier Li Peng declares martial law in parts of Beijing. The announcement leads to demonstrations all over China.

June 2, 1989 A new hunger strike is announced in Tiananmen Square. Some PLA troops start marching toward the square.

June 3, 1989 Troops surround Tiananmen Square. Some clashes take place in and around the square.

June 4, 1989 Crackdown. Tiananmen Square is emptied of students. Shooting and riots in the streets of Beijing.

August 1989 Poland ceases to be a communist country and holds democratic elections for its leaders.

October 1989 In response to demonstrations in many parts of China, the government passes a law controlling mass rallies and demonstrations.

November 1989 Deng Xiaoping retires from politics. Jiang Zemin becomes China's state president.

2001 A set of government documents on the events of 1989 are published in the West in *The Tiananmen Papers*.

In 1999 improvements costing twelve million dollars were made to Tiananmen Square. Here visitors flock to the newly reopened site.

Index